So You Want A
BABY?

AF885402

Charlotte H. Danciu, Esq.

Valuable information from an experienced Attorney
as you consider Adoption and Surrogacy

Consult a licensed, experienced Attorney. Avoid unlicensed agencies as you make these life changing decisions.

Copyright © 2022 by Charlotte H. Danciu, Esq.

All rights reserved. No part of this publication may be reproduced, distributed, or transmitted in any form or by any means, including photocopying, recording, or other electronic or mechanical methods, without the prior written permission of the publisher, except in the case of brief quotations embodied in critical reviews and certain other noncommercial uses permitted by copyright law. For permission requests, write to the publisher, addressed "Attention: Permissions Coordinator," at the address below.

Jacobs & Whitehall
21750 Hardy Oak Blvd
Suite 104 – 51700
San Antonio, Texas 78258
(888) 570-7338
www.jacobsandwhitehall.com

Ordering Information:

Quantity sales. Special discounts are available on quantity purchases by corporations, associations, and others. For details, contact the publisher at the address above.

Orders by U.S. trade bookstores and wholesalers. Please contact Jacobs & Whitehall: Tel: (888) 991-2766 or visit www.jacobsandwhitehall.com.

Printed in the United States of America

Published in 2022

DISCLAIMER

This publication is intended to be used for educational purposes only. No legal advice is being given, and no attorney-client relationship is intended to be created by reading this material. The author assumes no liability for any errors or omissions or for how this book or its contents are used or interpreted, or for any consequences resulting directly or indirectly from the use of this book. For legal or any other advice, please consult an experienced attorney or the appropriate expert, who is aware of the specific facts of your case and is knowledgeable in the law in your jurisdiction.

Adoption & Surrogacy

Charlotte H. Danciu, P.A.

1098 NW Boca Raton Boulevard
Boca Raton, FL 33432
www.adoption-surrogacy.com
(561) 300-6042

Testimonials

"We have been so blessed to have found such an honest and hard working group of people. From the beginning of our interaction with the lawyers and staff at Charlotte H. Danciu, PA you could tell that everyone was devoted to helping find families for children. It was very apparent that this was not just a job for the staff, that they genuinely cared for their birth families and wanted to support them the best way they could. They also took great care of the children and adoptive couples. Even after the placement of our son, I still receive phone calls and email from staff at Charlotte H. Danciu PA asking how we are adjusting and wanting to make sure we are doing well. We have referred several friends to Charlotte H. Danciu PA and would use them again in the future for another adoption."

— A Satisfied Client

****

"I once again had the honor to make a difference in a family's life. Doing this extraordinary life changing experience has its ups and downs but at the end of it all I found it was all worth it! Bringing an innocent or in my case two innocent lives into this world to a wonderful family has made me realize that even though you may be going through tough situations it doesn't mean you can't extend yourself to do something special for someone else. Things happen for a reason and you can only learn from what you have experienced. I not only did something special for this amazing family but doing it helped me realize in the end that I am strong and can do whatever I put my heart into. Congratulations to the Commissioning Couple with their two bundles of joy! I wish you well and may God continue to bless you and your family! It was my honor to help bring these twins into this world for your happiness. God works in mysterious ways."

— A Satisfied Client

****

"In the beginning, I didn't even know what a surrogate mother was. Once I discovered this outstanding procedure I knew it was something I had to do. I was informed of a family that had a sad but beautiful story and can no longer have children on their own. From the moment I was told their names, I knew they were family I was destined to do this for. After meeting them we grew together as one. Everything became natural as the process continued. We came to care for one another more and more. Although some people may think it is a long and difficult process, it actually isn't! This was the best gift I have given anyone and there is no gift better than an innocent child. I am pleased to say this process was a great one! I was able to work with an outstanding staff at Charlotte H. Danciu's office, where they ensured I was being taken care of and more. I delivered not one but two beautiful healthy baby girls for a beautiful and wonderful family! I am proud to be a surrogate mother!"

— A Satisfied Client

****

"The choice we made to adopt domestically versus internationally was based upon a strong recommendation of a friend who adopted through Charlotte's firm. When going on this kind of emotional journey you have to believe in the person/firm advocating for you. Charlotte has an uncanny ability to work with birth mothers and adoptive parents. Ours was an emotional journey that took may turns and twists but in the end we were paired with the baby meant for us. This process is not for the faint-hearted but if you are, believe in Charlotte and her team. We are an older couple of mixed race and on the journey of our lives with a child who doesn't know color. She just knows she is loved beyond belief."

— A Satisfied Client

****

"Charlotte Danciu is my hero. The adoption process can be so scary, but Charlotte made adopting my daughter Stephanie a dream come true. As far as I am concerned, choosing Charlotte Danciu to handle our adoption was a gift we gave ourselves."

— Sharry V.

****

"We would highly recommend working with the Law Offices of Charlotte H. Danciu. We matched within days of signing up with them! Maxine was always available to answer questions, provide reassurance, or just give support through our entire adoption process. Even though we worked primarily with Maxine, Charlotte was so supportive and caring to us as well. Both Charlotte and Maxine went above and beyond in the way they supported us and the birth parents from the time we matched until the time we brought our daughter home. Everyone in their office was friendly, professional, and always eager to answer any questions we had. The adoption process can be overwhelming at times, and it was so nice to have such a great group of people helping us build our family."

— A Satisfied Client

****

"Charlotte is an expert in the field, professional and reliable, as well as caring and compassionate. She helped our family complete two consecutive adoptions in Florida, and we highly recommend her services."

— Amanda F.

****

"We are so grateful for Charlotte, Maxine and the entire staff. They were always patient with our anxious hearts and showed their support with their quick responses to emails, texts and phone calls. Their knowledge helped us, first time adoptive parents, to understand the process and work through all the paperwork, financial situation, and the emotional parts too. We are truly blessed to have worked with such a great team. Through the good and the bad they were there for us! Thank you!"

– A Satisfied Client

****

"It is now 21 years since Charlotte helped my wife and I adopt our two children. Recently her office helped them locate and contact their respective birth moms. Charlotte's office has always been very helpful, understanding and open throughout the entire process. I very much recommend her and her staff to anyone wishing to adopt."

– C.O

****

Table of Contents

About The Author

I've been practicing family law since 1984, always focusing on children and helping to create families. I began with adoption, then around 1991, I started exploring other areas - surrogacy had just become popular. It started with egg donation, then evolved into surrogacy.

In my first case involving IFV in 1993, they put eight embryos in, hoping one would take - now they rarely put in more than one. What I see in my practice, for around 95% of my clients, IVF works on the first try. As reproductive endocrinologists started becoming more successful with the IVF process, my practice shifted from a few surrogacy cases to being my primary focus.

I saw a tremendous desire of families to have someone carry a baby for them that was genetically theirs. These families also desire to have more control over the child's health. With adoption, you don't have the same authority.

A lot of people adopt to save a child in the world, but many more adopt because they can't have a child of their own. With adoption, a birth mom will do what she has always done, and it may not be a healthy child when it's born. With surrogacy, you have control over those choices, and you have a genetic link to the child.

As the technology advanced, I saw the need for surrogacy grow. I've always been interested in obstetrics and the medical process of reproduction. At the time, nobody else was interested in practicing surrogacy law, as with my adoptions. As the practice evolved, I became involved with the legislative process in crafting the regulations for both adoption and surrogacy. No one else has contracts like I have, nor the experience.

Generally, it's an enjoyable practice. No matter what a surrogate mother gets paid, it's a tremendous sacrifice and a gift she gives this family. I look for clients that are mutually respectful of each other. If the intended parents don't appreciate this gift or indicate this is just a business deal and don't appreciate what this woman is doing for them, I won't work with them.

I love babies, children, and families. I love helping people become families. The personal rewards gained from helping with adoption and surrogacy are just tremendous. Watching the joy people get from adoption and surrogacy is amazing. I feel blessed to be practicing this area of law.

Becoming a Family Is Attainable

The miracle of having a child is possible, but you must do your research and go to the proper sources. Unfortunately, many unscrupulous people will take advantage of you. People are so desperate to be parents it makes it easier to be taken advantage of, especially with surrogacy.

In Florida, there is no licensing for surrogacy agencies. The only people licensed in surrogacy are lawyers. If you go to an agency, they have no license and therefore no accountability. I meet people that have sent $30,000 or $40,000 to some so-called agency and still don't have a surrogate 18 months later. It is terrible to take advantage of people when they are vulnerable.

If you're considering surrogacy or adoption, you need to go to someone reputable and ideally a licensed attorney. Other states may have licensing for agencies, but you should avoid going to an agency in Florida. You've already been through the pain of not being able to have a child. You don't need more pain added to the process. You need an attorney with experience helping people become families.

CHAPTER 1

SURROGACY VS. ADOPTION

Surrogacy and adoption can be for anyone; they can be single or married, same-sex or opposite-sex couples. Most of my surrogate and adoption clients come to me through referrals, either from a doctor or other people who have used my services.

With married opposite-sex couples, they've usually had several miscarriages or failures with in-vitro. Sometimes they already know they can't have children because of a medical reason, like the wife having had cancer. This is when I typically meet the family.

People looking to adopt come to me because they want a child, but they may not be able to afford the expensive assisted reproduction process of surrogacy. Or they want to adopt because they have always had it in their heart to take in a child that's already here.

Women who become surrogate mothers are not struggling. These are stable women. They are nurses, teachers, and stay-at-home moms with bachelors' degrees; women who have had a good pregnancy experience and have a secure life. Their number one reason for becoming a surrogate is to help someone else have a child.

These women have always thought about doing it. They feel there is no greater act on earth they could do for another human being, and benevolence is their number one reason. Of course, anybody can use the money, but usually, it's for things like finishing their master's degree, putting their own kids in private school, or for a down payment on their first home. It's not to pay the rent or get a divorce. These reasons differ with adoption, where the money received is for basic living expenses.

Whether adoption or surrogacy, it must be a woman with a big, unselfish heart who carries a child for someone else. In both cases, sacrifices are made. I am amazed to meet such incredible women that have the interest and courage to do this.

Surrogacy Options

There are two options for surrogacy in Florida, traditional and gestational surrogacy.

With traditional surrogacy, the egg of the surrogate is artificially inseminated. Although this option is legally permissible and tremendously less expensive, I do very few of these types of agreements. These are less common because the surrogate can keep the child at the end – biologically, it is her child. After the birth, she has 48 hours to rescind the consent of the surrogacy.

Gestational surrogacy is more popular, where families basically rent a womb. They use their own egg and sperm, or donor egg and sperm, or some combination of the two that does not include the surrogate's egg.

Before entering surrogacy, it is essential to do the research. First, ask yourself if you can afford it. It is an expensive process. Then, look for an experienced lawyer. Before hiring an attorney, ask, "How many surrogacy cases have you handled?" and "How long have you been practicing this type of law?"

When you find the right fit, let the lawyer advise you on your next steps. Let that person oversee the whole arrangement.

CHAPTER 2

SURROGACY: HOW TO GET STARTED

Once you find the right lawyer, you start the process by having a consultation to answer some key questions:

- What clinic do you want to use?
- What's important to you in your surrogate choice?
- What are your preferences regarding the relationship you will have with the surrogate?

- What are your medical views on difficult topics such as abortion, medical treatments, and vaccinations.

Once those questions are reviewed, we also discuss the expenses to ensure they can manage them.

From there, we look at the pool of surrogates in my practice. Unlike many other lawyers, I am a one-stop-shop. I find the surrogate for the family and legally represent them, but we get the surrogate her own attorney as well.

I personally interview all the surrogates we have. We do background checks, including flags for child abuse or criminal record, and talk to them about their views on life, medical opinions, and general outlook. I gather this information to introduce families to the surrogacy candidates.

Surrogacy Requirements in Florida

The surrogate candidate and the intended parents undergo a physical and psychological evaluation. The surrogate is more intensively assessed.

To qualify to be a surrogate mother in Florida, you must meet some basic requirements:

- Already have a child from an uncomplicated pregnancy.
- Demonstrate overall good health, with an acceptable body mass index (BMI).
- Be a U.S. citizen, green card holder, or other valid immigration status allowing you to remain in this country.

Generally, the surrogate's evaluation also involves a multi-phasic personality disorder test (MPPI).

The couple has to be healthy too. The FDA has medical guidelines for the materials implanted in the surrogate. For example, if the husband has Hepatitis C or a similar disease, it's highly unlikely to be transmitted from the embryo to the surrogate. The surrogate could waive this requirement and agree to use the sperm. There are ways around those things.

The couple's screening is more of a conference between the couple and the surrogate to ensure they are on the same page with challenging topics, like abortion. A psychologist usually addresses the issue by discussing hypothetical situations. For example, they might ask, "Say there is a medical complication and it's a choice between the surrogate's life or the baby's life...Whose life do you choose?"

Some couples are surprised by the evaluation results, but it depends on which psychologist they see. As long as the couple doesn't have a criminal or child abuse background, I don't care how they plan to raise the child – it's their business. Some psychologists think differently. They seem to enjoy the power of deciding who should and shouldn't have a baby. I don't work with those so into it that they act as God, deciding who can have a child.

Couples can be frustrated by these psychologists. Their doctor may have a favorite psychologist and send them to that psychologist or whatever language. I try to steer my clients towards the psychologists doing what's recommended by the American Society for Reproductive Medicine. (ASRM).

Surrogacy Terms

I write my contracts very straightforward, using plain English or Spanish - whatever language the parties speak—but they cover everything. For example, what if the couple goes down in a plane crash before the baby is born? Who gets the baby? We set up a guardianship designation for this. What if the surrogate is in an accident, on life support, at just 27 weeks of pregnancy? The doctor says she is brain dead, but they could keep her alive for another couple of weeks gestation. For this instance, we have the surrogate establish a living will so her significant other will keep her alive in the worst-case scenario.

When people walk into surrogacy, they have no idea. They are not thinking about the tough hard questions that could come up that these contracts address. The surrogate must be advised to have her own attorney, and the couple will pay for it. She has the right to waive the representation as well.

CHAPTER 3

FINDING A SURROGACY MATCH

To find a great surrogate match, you have to do a massive amount of networking. It's tough to find qualified candidates. It takes an experienced practitioner like me to screen out the issues. You have to know the red flags.

When someone comes to you and says they don't have custody of their kids, but it was by mutual agreement, I want to dig into this further.

I have people come to me with surrogates they've found through an agency or on their own who do not have a green card. I say, "She might be a lovely young Guatemalan housekeeper, who needs the money, but if she leaves your house one day to go to the grocery store and is picked up and deported, you will never get your baby out of Guatemala."

I get referrals from other surrogates I have worked with and find surrogates on the various surrogate websites and blogs online. I have a good reputation with them. They know I'm not going to shortchange them or match them with people who will not treat them well.

Then matching the surrogate with the family is based on the family's preferences. People have different thoughts concerning relationships, eating organic or kosher, vaccinations, etc. In our consultation, every family has distinct priorities that I narrow down and then look through what I have.

Finding surrogate candidates can be challenging. I talk to about 20 a month and usually settle on just one or two – sometimes it's different. With the pandemic last year, I had a lot of new surrogates, perhaps because everyone was home. I also had a lot because nobody was commissioning them to carry babies. People were afraid to start families during the pandemic.

When families can't handle the cost of surrogacy, I may suggest looking to a close friend or family member. It is a lot less expensive. Upfront, you have to know there will be no closure at the end like when a stranger carries for you. Some people don't want to always recognize that Aunt Suzy was your surrogate mother.

That tie doesn't bother everyone. I've had sisters that carry for sisters, and friends carry for friends. It all depends on your relationship. In this situation, it is ideal that you know and trust the person and have a high comfort level with them. Many families eventually tell the child they had a surrogate mother help them to be born. The difference is when it's your sister or friend, everyone knows it from the beginning, and the child will learn early on.

Surrogate Agencies and Attorneys

If you work with an agency in Florida, you must also use an attorney. The surrogacy agency can't do the legal work. What a surrogacy agency typically does is just find surrogates for people. You have to be careful using agencies; there is no licensing or regulation, they are not attorneys and do not know the law.

I don't often work with agencies; they tend to prefer to work with inexpensive attorneys who attorneys who just use "cookie cutter" contracts and stay out of the process. But they absolutely need to have an attorney to do the legal work. When people come to me after finding a surrogate through an agency, usually that is all they do. They find the surrogate and then are gone. I do the rest.

Ideally, you should find a reputable attorney from the very beginning when you decide to go the surrogacy route. You don't need an agency. You can work with an attorney, such as myself, who also finds a qualified Surrogate. I have accountability to the Florida Bar. I am licensed and regulated. You know if you give me money, you will either get a surrogate or your money back. That doesn't happen with agencies.

When searching for an attorney, you want to ensure you find the best fit. Questions to ask before hiring a surrogacy attorney include:

- What is your experience with surrogacy?
- How many cases have you handled?
- Is this the primary focus of your practice?
- Are you going to be handling it, or will you pass it off to others?
- How available are you in the process? Can I get a hold of you?

CHAPTER 4

SURROGACY PROCESS: START TO FINISH

It's not required, but recommended, that the intended parents and surrogate mothers have their own legal representation. Each parent doesn't need an attorney when they are a couple. The intending parents, as a couple, have me, and we recommend an attorney outside of my firm represent the surrogate.

The attorney who represents the intended parents cannot also represent the surrogate. The surrogate does have the option of not having an attorney. Like in some cases, when the intended parents know the surrogate, such as a sister or friend, they do not anticipate any kind of conflict of interest. It is right in the contract that it is recommended and I can't advise her on it. However, she can waive having an attorney.

Once the couple has chosen their surrogate and she has been medically approved, I draw up the surrogacy contract between the intended family and the surrogate. If the surrogate is married, the spouse must also sign the contract. The agreement must be executed before starting any medication in the in-vitro cycle process.

This contract can be amended later, as long as it's in writing. Sometimes we have couples who have lived together for years but never married. They want to have a baby now, and they don't want to go through a second or stepparent adoption. We will start out with one intended parent on the contract, and when they get married, we amend the agreement to add the second person.

Another example is a surrogate who ends up with a very complicated pregnancy and needs more money for childcare for her own children. If the parties mutually agree, we do an amendment. Or, if the surrogate doesn't get pregnant in a year, we can modify the contract to do an extension.

Surrogate and Intended Family Rights and Contact

Intended families and surrogates have a lot of interaction. Most of my surrogates are in Florida, but I have clients worldwide. Everybody communicates at least once a week.

If they live close by, they'll go to doctor's visits. If they live out of town, often they attend appointments over the phone or Facetime. When I have clients out of the country, often they will come for the big ultrasound at 20 weeks.

Most surrogates are open to whatever interaction the family wants somewhat more than others.

The contract is executed to protect the rights of the intended family and the surrogate. Although the surrogate agrees for the intended family to know all about her and her medical history, she still has a right to privacy. If she is getting an examination and asks them to leave the room, they have to go. The one legal right the surrogate doesn't have is to keep the child when it is born.

The intended family has the right to get their child and the right to enforce the contract if the surrogate is not following the agreement. If she doesn't go to the doctor, doesn't eat well, or gets a DUI, they can go to arbitration, mediation, or court to require her to abide by the contract. The intended family also has an obligation to compensate the surrogate and fulfill the other provisions as required by the contract.

Intended Family Liability

My surrogacy contract addresses the inherent risks that could occur with pregnancy, both medically and psychologically. Thankfully, we have never had a surrogate suffer because of a pregnancy. But the contract does address the possibilities, and she assumes the risk.

I do provide in my contracts that, if needed, the intended parents will pay for counseling and therapy for up to eight weeks after the delivery. I try not to select women who express any reservations or hesitation. If they say something like, "I know it will be really hard at the end, but I think I can do it," I tell them they are not the right candidate.

As the surrogate, you must go in from the beginning knowing you are the incubator. You have to have a clinical approach. If you think you will get attached or need counseling to get through this, then I don't believe that you are a good candidate.

CHAPTER 5

TERMS OF A SURROGACY AGREEMENT

The contract I provide clients covers what is considered acceptable and unacceptable behavior. The surrogate agrees to share information about the pregnancy. She also agrees to not engage in reckless, irresponsible, or contra-indicated activities, such as riding a horse, getting her nails done with formaldehyde, coloring her hair, drinking alcohol, smoking cigarettes, visiting high crime areas, or not evacuating during a hurricane. If she meets someone while pregnant, perhaps a new boyfriend, they will have a screening before they are sexually active since their private actions could potentially expose the baby to infection. She agrees to a lot of things in the contract.

Once the contract is signed and pregnancy established, there is basically no backing out of the agreement. The contract spells out when there can be a legitimate termination, but it can't just be from either side that you don't want to do it anymore. It costs a lot of money even to screen a surrogate. The contract indicates the surrogate will make three attempts, typically over one year.

You don't want to spend $10,000 screening a surrogate, and after one attempt, she tries to back out of the agreement. So, that would be a breach to quit. At the same time, you don't really want to force somebody to go through with surrogacy if they don't want to. If the surrogate doesn't make the two additional attempts, she must pay the intended parents back all the money paid to screen her.

There have been cases where the intended couple has split up, and the husband claims he never wanted to go through the process in the first place, saying, "I'm not paying child support." Yes, he is paying child support. Courts have ruled that the intended parents have commissioned the surrogate to have this baby, and they are responsible for it when it is born.

For the most part, the agreement ends after the birth, when all parties sign all the required paperwork and the surrogate has been compensated for her time. Some features of the contract continue into perpetuity – meaning forever. Conditions that continue may include the surrogate will have no contact with the child without permission.

Surrogacy Payment

The law says surrogate mothers cannot be paid a fee for carrying the child. They can only be paid reasonable living expenses and compensation for the convenience of the pregnancy. The overall cost range is broad and varies depending on the situation, such as a first-time or repeat surrogate.

In my practice, the base minimum I see is $35,000 to $65,000. If the surrogate has done this before, she is often compensated at a higher base. Some people want someone who has been a surrogate before because they know she is familiar with the process. Her living expenses may be more because this will impact her life for at least a year. Some people think this is a lot of money, but if you calculate something that must be done 24/7 for ten months, those are actually pretty low wages.

Typically, in my practice, a surrogate will get a $2,500 to $3,000 retainer to go through the IVF. Once a heartbeat is established, usually four weeks after transfer, I, acting as escrow agent, will begin paying her monthly. The sum of that check increases as she gets further along in the pregnancy. It might start as $1,000 per month upon confirmation of pregnancy, going up to $1,500 a month at 12 weeks, $2,000 a month at 16 weeks, etc., throughout the pregnancy.

CHAPTER 6

WORKING WITH A SURROGACY ATTORNEY

I have over 35 years of experience helping people become families, more than 25 of those years as a surrogacy attorney. I have seen a lot of different scenarios, and I have not found a crisis that was not fixable. I devour information on surrogacy, keeping me up to date and effectively communicating with doctors. I have both years of legal experience and years of being immersed in the medical aspect of surrogacy.

My knowledge helps me easily discuss any issue that may come up in the process.

It's scary when you are trusting someone else to carry your child. It's like when you are not too sure about using a babysitter when the kids can't tell you if something goes wrong. With an unborn baby, anything the surrogate does will impact the child and impact you for the rest of your life. I understand this. At the same time, some intended families act as if they own the surrogate. They have to respect she has a life too. I end up being not only an attorney but a mediator, helping to facilitate their communication.

To be successful, there needs to be a good match made from the beginning on both sides. I am very good at ruling out candidates to have a smooth surrogacy journey free of issues.

INDEX

S

NOTES